Mindfulness for Beginners

Live in the Moment without Stress and Worry!

Learn to live a Happy and Fulfilling Life!

Enjoy Every Moment of Your Life!

Table of Contents

Introduction

I want to thank you and congratulate you for downloading the book, *"Mindfulness for Beginners: Live in the Moment without Stress and Worry! Learn to Live a Happy and Fulfilling Life! Enjoy Every Moment of Your Life"*.

Do you think about the future often or do you have a tendency to dwell on the past? Do you often zone out or daydream? Do you often worry about things that don't even matter? Do you routinely relive an embarrassing memory?

It's a common knowledge that worrying is a symptom of an anxiety disorder. But, surprisingly, daydreaming is also a symptom of anxiety and depression. Thinking about the past or the future turns off some parts of your brain. This is the reason why you tend to forget things when you're worrying or day dreaming. Thinking about the future or the past too much can wreak havoc in your life. It can keep you from enjoying the little things and joys in life. It can keep you from noticing awesome everyday things. Worrying or daydreaming too often can make you feel like you are sleepwalking through life. Five to ten years from now, you wouldn't have any idea where your years went. Not living in the present moment can drain your energy. It also keeps you from catching key information. It reduces your productivity, compassion, and gratitude. It also stops you from living fully.

So, if you want to live a fulfilling and happy life, you have to enjoy every moment of it. Living in the moment can improve your life in many ways. It can:

- Take the edge off and reduce physical pain.

- It allows you to control your cravings and enjoy your food.

- It gets things done so it improves your productivity.

- It helps you learn new things.

- It helps you appreciate the little things in life.

- It improves your creativity.

- It allows you to establish healthier and mutually respectful relationships.

- It allows you to be connected with your surroundings and with life, in general.

- It creates strong feelings of inner peace and strength.

- It improves the level of your happiness.

This book contains tips and strategies that will help you practice mindfulness in your daily life. You'll learn how to practice mindfulness through meditation. You'll also learn how to incorporate mindfulness techniques in your daily tasks such as eating, walking, or even brushing your teeth. This book also answers frequently asked questions about mindfulness and contains tips that will help you jumpstart your meditation practice.

Mindfulness or living in the present moment can change your life on different levels. It can improve your relationships, your career, and even it can even expedite your personal growth. So, if you're feeling like life passes you by, it's time to take matters into your own hands and start living in the present moment. Soon, you'll see positive changes in your life. You'll be happier, more grounded, and more fulfilled. When you live in the present moment, the world becomes your playground.

Thanks again for downloading this book, I hope you enjoy it!

The trademarks that are used are without any consent, and the publication of the trademark is without permission or backing by the trademark owner. All trademarks and brands within this book are for clarifying purposes only and are the owned by the owners themselves, not affiliated with this document.

Chapter 1:
Mindfulness 101

Mindfulness practice is getting more and more popular nowadays, especially in the field of psychology. More and more mental health professionals recommend the daily practice of mindfulness to their patients. However, mindfulness is not a new concept. In fact, it has been around for 2,500 years.

Mindfulness is the core element Buddhist practices such as Vipassana, anapanasati, and sattipatthana. Dr. Jon Kabat-Zinn popularized it in the West when he developed the MBSR or Mindfulness-based Stress Reduction technique. This technique is now widely used by medical professionals, hospitals, medical centers, and health maintenance organizations. Kabat-Zinn learned the mindfulness technique from Zen masters like Seung Sahn and Thich Nhat Hanh.

What is mindfulness, really? Well, mindfulness is the gentle effort to be incessantly present with experience. Mindfulness is paying attention with purpose. It is a state of open and active attention to the present moment. When you are being mindful, you observe your actions, feelings, and thoughts from a distance without judgment.

The regular practice of meditation has a number of scientifically backed benefits, including:

Mindfulness lowers stress.

Research shows that mindfulness can reduce stress substantially. It helps control the production of stress hormones called cortisol.

It helps you know yourself more.

Mindfulness meditation helps you get to know yourself more. It helps you objectively analyze yourself and it helps you get to know your feelings more.

It improves your cognitive function.

Studies show that practicing mindfulness meditation on a regular basis helps improve your cognitive function. A research shows that college students who practiced mindfulness scored better in the GRE than those who did not.

A study conducted in 2010 also shows that mindfulness help improve the memory. This study shows the military officers who practiced mindfulness have better memory than those who didn't.

A study conducted at the University of California – Los Angeles shows that people who practice mindfulness meditation for more than a year has bigger amounts of gyrification, or the folds in the brain's cortex. These extra folds help practitioners process information faster than regular folks. These extra folds also improve your decision-making skills.

It helps you focus.

Mindfulness is best for people with ADHD mainly because it helps them focus. So, if constant daydreaming is keeping you from functioning well and completing your daily task, then you should start your meditation practice.

It helps you empathize with others.

It's no secret that people who practice mindfulness (like the Dalai Lama) are more compassionate and more emphatic than others are. A study conducted in 2008 shows that responders who practiced mindfulness meditation are more compassionate. This is because mindfulness promotes activity in the regions of the brain that are linked to empathy.

It keeps your mind young and vibrant.

A study conducted at Beth Israel Deaconess Medical Center shows that mindfulness meditation slows down the progression of age-related disorders such as dementia and Alzheimer's.

It improves your mental health.

Mindfulness helps people accept their painful emotions and experiences. It helps people gain perspective on maladaptive, self-defeating, and irrational thoughts. It helps ease a number of mental health issues, including substance abuse, depression, couple's conflicts, eating disorder, anxiety disorder, and obsessive compulsive disorder.

Meditation also improves your mood. It helps build resilience and it keeps you from becoming overly emotional when exposed to challenging and stressful situations. To prove this, a study was conducted on Lama Oser, the Dalai Lama's right hand man. He's been practicing meditation for more than 30 years. They scanned Lama Oser's brain using an MRI scanner and compared his results with over 100 different people. The results were astounding. Lama Oser's pre-frontal cortex activity ratio indicates high levels of well-being, equanimity, and resilience.

It improves creativity.

Divergent thinking and convergent thinking determines one's level of creativity. Divergent thinking allows you to come up with different ideas and convergent thinking helps you solidify those ideas into powerful concepts. A study conducted in Leiden university shows that mindfulness meditation significantly improves both convergent and divergent thinking.

It improves your overall health.

Studies show that mindfulness helps improve your physical health. It lowers down your blood pressure, it reduces chronic pain, it improves the function of your digestive system, and it also improves sleep.

It enhances your overall well-being.

Mindfulness helps you pay attention to the little things in life so it increases your life satisfaction. It helps you savor the little pleasures in life and help you deal with adversities and problems in a healthy way. It also increases your self-esteem and self-confidence.

Mindfulness also allows you to connect with others. It helps you improve your patience and tolerance, so it improves the quality of your relationships. It also reduces the feelings of loneliness and sadness.

It's free.

Most of the time, practicing mindfulness is free. So, this is a cost effective way to fight stress, anxiety, and other mental diseases.

The regular practice of mindfulness can improve the quality of your life. It can improve the level of your happiness. It also improves your social skills and helps you connect with others in a more meaningful way. Mindfulness makes you feel more alive.

Frequently Asked Questions

If you're a beginner, a number of questions may come up in your mind. You may have doubts about meditation. You may wonder if mindfulness is the best stress reduction technique for you. Here are the answers to frequently asked questions about mindfulness practice:

Do I have to be spiritual to practice meditation?

No. It is a secular type of meditation and it is for everyone.

Do I have to enroll in a class?

It's better to enroll in the class, especially if you're serious with your mindfulness meditation practice. But, you can practice meditation by yourself. The tips and techniques contained in this book should be enough to help you jump start your mindfulness practice.

Can kids practice the mindfulness techniques, too?

Yes, absolutely! Kids can benefit from mindfulness meditation practice, too.

How long before I'll notice the results?

Mindfulness is a relaxation technique. So, you'll reap its stress-reduction benefits right away. However, it will take a while for you to reap the other benefits of mindfulness, such as improved cognitive function and physical health. The results of meditation are highly variable. This means that people who practice meditation may encounter different results. But, most people can already see the change in their life after a couple of weeks.

Do I have to sit down when I'm practicing mindfulness?

No. In this book, you'll find different techniques that will allow you to practice mindfulness in your daily life. You can practice mindfulness while you are doing your report or while brushing your teeth.

How can paying attention to simple activities like brushing my teeth help me?

Most of us go through life on an autopilot. Most of us walk from point A to point B without even noticing how we did it. We sometimes develop a habit or ruminating about the past or projecting about the future that we forget to focus on the present moment. Practicing mindfulness while you are doing simple activities like brushing your teeth will help you pay attention on the present moment. You begin to interact and process each experience as it is and this could create amazing changes in your life.

I do not have time to practice mindfulness meditation, what can I do?

It is best to set aside a few minutes of your time for this practice. But, if you're too busy, you can incorporate your meditation practice into your daily life. You can practice mindfulness while you are eating, while you are typing, or while you are working out. In this book, you'll learn the simple mindfulness practice that will allow you to practice mindfulness while performing your daily task.

Is mindfulness just a new age fad?

No, it's not a fad. It's something that you can practice for a couple of years and even for decades. Buddhist monks and spiritual mystics have practiced mindfulness for centuries.

Is mindfulness for me?

Mindfulness is for everyone; your age, status, race, location, or job does not matter. Everyone can benefit from it. It can improve your mental health and it can also help you cope with life. Mindfulness also helps make the most out of your potential.

Do I have to meditate every day?

Yes, especially if you want to reap the full benefits of mindfulness. Studies show that regular mindfulness meditation can help reshape your brain. Regular practice helps improve your cognitive function and it increases your emotional intelligence over time. It also improves your decision-making and people skills.

How long should I meditate?

You can start with three minutes a day during your first week of mindfulness practice. You could gradually increase your practice to 10 to 20 minutes. Then, after a few months of practice, you can increase your mindfulness meditation technique for 30 minutes to one hour;

experiment and check what works well for you.

I am a restless person and I cannot sit still. Can I still practice mindfulness meditation?

Many people think that only those who have a calm and tranquil mind can practice mindfulness meditation, but the truth is that those who have restless minds can reap the most benefits from it. Mindfulness helps you pay attention to everything that you're experiencing, may it be physical pain, restlessness, emotions, or difficult feelings. Movement mindfulness is the best option for you if you have a restless mind. Also, it's a good idea to practice under the supervision of a meditation master. Your teacher can teach you specific techniques that address your specific needs.

Do I have to sit in a lotus position to do mindfulness meditation?

No, you can sit on a chair or a cushion in whatever position that's comfortable for you. You can even practice mindfulness meditation while standing up, moving, or lying down.

I have been struggling with mental health problems for years. Is mindfulness practice suitable for me?

Well, even though mindfulness is for everyone, people who have pre-existing mental health issues should only practice specific types of mindfulness meditation. If your mental health problem is relatively mild then you can simply practice the basic mindfulness meditation techniques for at least eight weeks. However, if you have serious mental health issues such as psychosis, anxiety, and depression, then you can talk to your therapist and try

MBCT or mindfulness-based cognitive therapy.

Why do people practice mindfulness?

Different people practice mindfulness for different reasons. But here are the common reasons why people practice mindfulness:

- Stress reduction

- Depression

- Insomnia or sleep disruption

- Difficulty with concentration or focus

- Anxiety

- Chronic pain

- Substance abuse recovery

- The desire to live consciously and more fully

When you practice mindfulness, do you think about nothing?

No. Mindfulness does not and will not stop you from thinking. It simply allows you to notice your thoughts.

Can I practice mindfulness meditation alone or should I attend a class?

Yes, you can practice mindfulness meditation alone. You do not have to enroll in a class. But, if you have a restless mind or you are suffering from serious mental health issues, it's best to practice under the supervision of a teacher or a meditation master.

Is mindfulness the same with meditation?

Mindfulness is a type of meditation, just like other meditation techniques such as Kundalini meditation and Mantra meditation.

Tips for Beginners

Here are some of the tips that you can use to jumpstart your meditation practice:

Commit to it.

To reap the maximum benefits of mindfulness, you have to commit to it and practice regularly. You have to set aside a couple of hours of your day for your mindfulness. List it as part of your daily "to do" list and make sure that it's part of your daily schedule.

Start your day with mindfulness practice.

You can do your mindfulness practice anytime, but if you're a beginner, it's best to do this in the morning right after waking up or before leaving for work. This is because your mind is easier to tame in the morning before you begin your work and other daily activities. But, as you progress, you can start practicing mindfulness anytime you wish. You can practice while eating lunch or at night before sleeping.

Let go.

To live in the moment, you have to learn to let go of any distracting thoughts. This may be hard to do at first, but after weeks of mindfulness practice, this will become easier and more natural.

Learn to slow down.

In these modern times, people have to multi-task and do many things at the same time. But, to fully live in the moment, you must learn to slow down and calm your body and mind. When you talk to other people, try to pay attention to each word. When you're typing, pay attention to the sound of the keyboard as you hit each key.

Be patient.

Mindfulness practice is not easy. It will take you weeks, months, or even years to master it so you have to be patient with yourself and just keep going. But, as the days or weeks go by, you'll gradually experience positive changes in your life. You'll feel more relaxed and more alive.

Have fun.

A lot of people think that mindfulness practice is boring. This is not true. Mindfulness is the act of being present so it is actually fun and exciting. As mentioned earlier, living in the present moment is not as easy as most people think. So, you just have to enjoy the process. Once your mind is settled in, you'll reap the full benefits of mindfulness and you'll realize that your reality is even ten times better than your day dreams.

Do not give up.

If you have difficulty taming your thoughts or sitting still even for a couple of minutes, don't give up and immediately decide that mindfulness meditation is not right for you. The path to mindfulness is not an easy process. If you have a hard time sitting still, you're the type of person who needs mindfulness practice the most.

Mindfulness is an inexpensive way to improve the quality of your life. It improves your concentration and cognitive skills. It improves your work performance and most importantly, it increases the level of your happiness. Mindfulness is not an easy practice. To reap its full benefits, you need to be committed to it. You need to practice mindfulness regularly to master it, and once you do, you'll realize that it is worth all the effort.

Chapter 2:
Basic Mindfulness Meditation Technique or Vipassana Meditation

People from Western countries usually use this most basic meditation technique. This technique helps relieve stress. It also promotes self-acceptance and it improves your cognitive function. This practice is also perfect for beginners as it is quite simple and easy to do.

Before you begin this practice, it's important that you wear comfortable clothes. Also, do this in a place or a room where you will not be disturbed. Turn off your mobile phone and all other distractions. You can also light some incense sticks or scented candles to enhance your experience. It can also help if you do some stretching exercises or do some yoga poses before starting. This will condition your body so it will be easier for you to focus. It's also important to set an alarm. This allows you to focus on your practice without having to check the clock. Remember that it takes a while to reap the benefits of mindfulness meditation so it's important that you're committed to it. You have to set aside a couple of minutes every day for your mindfulness meditation practice.

- Sit in a comfortable position. You can sit on a chair or you can sit on the floor in a cross legged position. Do not lie down as you may fall asleep during the process.

- Close your eyes and take deep breaths. Inhale through your nose and exhale through your mouth.

- As you breathe in, say silently "inhaling". As you breathe out, say silently "exhaling".

- Try to focus only on your breath.

- It is likely that you will get some distracting thoughts, especially when you have an untrained mind. You may think about something trivial like food or movies. When this happens, simply acknowledge these thoughts and then bring your focus back to your breath. You may have to do this many times, especially during your first few sessions.

- Once you hear the alarm. Say a silent prayer of gratitude and open your eyes.

This technique is one of the exercises used in Dr. Kabat-Zinn's MBSR or Mindfulness-Based Stressed Reduction program. This technique helps relax your body and it also strengthens your mind.

You can do this in your bedroom or in the office. You can do this technique any time of the day, but when you're still jumpstarting your meditation practice, it is important to do this in the morning as your mind is still fresh and a lot easier to control. You can do this for about 3-5 minutes during your first week and you can increase your mindfulness meditation practice by a few minutes as you progress. Most Zen masters do this for more than 3 hours a day!

Chapter 3:
The Body Scan Technique

The body scan practice is also one of the more popular forms of mindfulness commonly practiced in hospitals and rehabilitation centers. This technique establishes a stronger mind-body connection. This will help you become more alert, and yet you will feel more relaxed.

You can practice this technique while lying down, but if you're sitting, try to maintain a straight back. So, to begin, place both of your hands on your thighs. Relax your shoulders and then close your eyes. Place your arms on your side. Do not slouch. If you're lying down, keep your back straight.

- Take a few deep breaths. Inhale through your nose and exhale through your mouth. Breathe high into your nostrils and try to expand your chest and then release your breath through your mouth. Observe your chest rising and dropping each time you take a breath. Pay attention to the sound of your breath. Do this around 20 times to get your mind and body in a relaxed state. Pay attention to your breath. Is it fast? Is it slow?

- Now, try to let go of any tension in your body. Try to breathe out all the tension in your body as you exhale. Just stay still and pay attention to your breathing.

- Now, shift your attention from your breath to your forehead and to the top of your head. Do you feel any discomfort in your head and forehead? Notice any sensations in that area of your body. Do you feel a tingling sensation on your head? Does it feel hot or cool? Can you feel any tension? Does it feel itchy? Just take time to notice these sensations.

- Then, shift your attention to the back of your head. Do you feel an itch on the back of your head? Do you feel any tension? What are the sensations that you feel?

- Move your attention to your neck. Take time to notice the skin on your neck. Notice any itching or burning sensation in your neck. Do you feel some tension in that area of your body?

- Then, shift your attention to your shoulder. Do you notice any tension or ache? What are the sensations that you feel in your shoulders? Notice how your shoulder moves as you inhale and exhale.

- Bring your attention to your arms. Take time to notice each arm. Notice any pain or ache in that region of your body. Do you feel muscle spasms? Do you feel burning sensations in your arms?

- Draw your attention to your left elbow and take time to notice the skin on your elbow? Is it dark? Take time to examine the lines on your elbow. Do you feel any sensation on your elbow? Do you feel any tension? Then, shift your attention to your wrists and then to your hands. Pay attention to each finger. Feel the deep muscles in your hands.

- Then, notice your back. Watch the movement of your back as you breathe. Then, move your attention to your buttocks. Give your buttocks your full attention even for a moment. Then, move your awareness to your pelvis and then to the muscle of your thighs. Pay attention to those muscles. Do you feel any sensation? Is it relaxed? Do you feel any tension or pain on your thighs.

- Then, take time to notice your knees. Bring your full attention to each knee and then move your gaze to your calves. Do you feel any tension on your calves? Do they feel heavy? Notice any pain and then move your full attention to your feet. Do you feel any burning sensation or itchiness on your feet? Take time to notice the contact of your soles to the ground. Does it feel cold or warm? If you're wearing shoes, are your shoes loose or tight?

- Turn your attention to your whole body. How does your body feel? Do you feel good about your body? Are you experiencing any pain or tension? Then, bring your focus back to your breath. Pay attention to how your chest rises and collapses as you breathe. During this process, distracting thoughts will enter your mind – trivial thoughts, thoughts of better days, and even worries. When this happens, simply acknowledge those thoughts and then let those thoughts go. Bring your focus back to your breath. Bring your focus back to the present moment.

To improve your cognitive function and health, it is important that you do this exercise on a daily basis. Do this exercise for 3-10 minutes daily, and in just a few weeks, you'll see amazing results. You'll feel healthier, happier, and more alive.

Chapter 4:
Walking Meditation

Walking meditation is a great because it allows you to move. This technique is perfect for people who have a hard time sitting still. Walking meditation is not the same as strolling in the park. Walking meditation requires you to focus on your feet as you move. You also get to hit two birds with one stone as you get to meditate and exercise at the same time. This type of meditation is invigorating, interesting, and it is fun too.

Here's how you can do walking meditation:

1. Stretch and do a couple of warm up exercise before you begin your meditation practice. You can stretch your legs or your arms. You can do a few yoga poses like the Warrior Pose or the Downward Dog to help stretch your body.

2. Then, stand still for a minute or two. Take deep breaths. Watch your chest go up and down as you breathe in and breathe out. Take time to notice the sensations in your body, especially in your leg area.

3. Then, start walking. Pay attention to each of your steps. As soon as your foot touches the ground, take note of any feelings or sensations. Then, as you lift your foot, again take time to notice the sensations.

4. You'll discover that you feel different types of feelings each time you make a step. There's a different sensation that comes with every step. Remember to notice only the feelings and sensation and refrain from making any judgments.

5. When distracting thoughts enter your mind during your walking meditation session, simply

acknowledge them and then gently shift your focus back to your steps.

You can do this for 10 to 15 minutes. You can walk around the neighborhood or in your local park. You can do this alone and you can do this in groups. As with other forms of mindfulness, you need to do this daily to reap its full results.

Chapter 5:
The Heart of the Rose Meditation Technique

This is one of the most popular mindfulness meditation techniques in the west. Buddhist monks have been practicing this technique for centuries, but Robin Sharma introduced this to the west through his book, "The Monk Who Sold His Ferrari". This technique is a form of mindful awareness. It helps you pay attention to details. This technique also helps you live in the present moment.

For this exercise, you'll need a rose or any type of flower.

- Sit in a comfortable position and how the flower. Then take deep breaths. Inhale through your nose and exhale through your mouth. As you inhale and exhale, notice how your chest goes up and down with every breath.

- After ten breaths, shift your attention to the rose. What's the color of the rose? Is it red, white, or yellow? Is it fresh or is it wilting? Is it small or is it large. Take time to notice all the petals. Do you see lines on the petals? Take time to appreciate each curve and each petal.

- Then, shift your attention to the center of the rose. What can you see? Pay attention to each curve. Notice each petal curled up to the center of the flower. Just stare at the center of the rose for three to five minutes. If a distracting thought enters your mind, acknowledge that thought and gently release it without judgment.

- Then, after your meditation time, say a silent prayer of gratitude and then go about your day.

This technique is difficult, especially if you have an untrained or a restless mind. This will take you a couple of weeks to master so you have to be patient with yourself. You can also set an alarm so that you don't have to look at the clock while you are doing the practice. You can do this for two to three minutes for the first few minutes and then you can increase your meditation time as you progress.

The Heart of the Rose meditation technique is challenging, but it is very beneficial. It helps reduce stress and tension in your body. This technique also sharpens your mind and improves your critical thinking and decision-making skills. This mindfulness practice also helps increase emotional intelligence and it is an effective way to alleviate the symptoms of anxiety.

Chapter 6:
Mindful Eating

Mindful eating helps you lose weight. It also helps control cravings and it promotes healthy eating habits. So, if you're prone to overeating, this is the perfect mindfulness technique for you. Many weight loss programs and fitness professionals have been using this technique for years. Mental health professionals also use this technique to help people with eating disorders.

Mindful eating empowers you to make healthy choices. It teaches you to distinguish real hunger from cravings. It also helps develop self-trust and it is an effective weight management tool.

Here's how you can practice mindful eating:

- Express your gratitude before the meal.

- Before you eat, it is important to honor the food by expressing your gratitude during the meal. You can say a prayer of gratitude, but if you're not the spiritual type, you can simply look at your food and silently thank the farmers that grew the lettuce in your salad or the chef who prepared your meal.

- Do not watch TV while eating.

- It is important to eat at the dining table and not in front of your TV, computer, or in your car. Also, when you're eating with others, do not talk about work.

- Engage all of your senses when eating your meal.

- Before you wolf down that plate of pasta, take time to notice the colors and the textures of your food. Then, one by one, take time to notice all the ingredients – the cream, the tomato sauce, the tomatoes, the meat, and the noodles. Does your food look attractive or appetizing? What do you think of the food presentation?

- Then, eat like a food critic. Take time to notice the flavors and the different spices. Notice the taste of the pasta as if it's the first time that you've tasted it. You also need to engage your sense of smell. Does your food smell good?

- Chew Thoroughly

- You have to savor each small bits and chew thoroughly. It can help you slow down and experience fully the taste of your food. Also, make sure to chew thoroughly and avoid overeating. You have to eat in reasonable portions. While you are eating, observe your body carefully and stop eating once you feel full.

Remember that eating is a sacred ceremony. It is a process of nourishing and honoring your body by feeding it with the necessary nutrients. So, honor your meal time. Avoid eating in front of the computer or in front of the TV. Remember that each meal is a blessing so learn to give that meal the attention that it deserves.

Chapter 7:
Mindfulness in Your Daily Life

The mindfulness technique allows you to incorporate mindfulness into your daily tasks. It helps develop heightened awareness and it helps increase your appreciation of your daily task. If you go about your day on an auto-pilot, this activity will help increase your awareness of your daily tasks and activities. Here's how you can practice mindfulness in your daily life:

1. While brushing your teeth.

You can still practice mindfulness while doing a mundane task like brushing your teeth. Pay attention to the color of your toothpaste. Is it blue, red, or white? Do you see mint crystals? Does it have a jelly-like texture? Then, as you brush your teeth, pay attention to the sensations in your month/ Do you feel a warm sensation? Can you feel any mouth sores? How does the toothpaste taste? Is it sweet or is it minty? Notice how the brush feels on your teeth and your tongue. Take time to notice the motions of the brush. Then, as you wash your mouth with water, take time to notice how the water feels in your mouth. Is it warm or cold? Does it feel good? Do you feel any discomfort?

Doing this experience, you will help increase your awareness of your own tasks and experiences. Do this exercise every day and you'll be surprised with the result.

2. While working.

If you have an office job and you use a computer 99% of the time while you're in the office, then do "mindful typing". Before you start typing, take time to pay attention to your surroundings. What's the color of your personal computer? What's the color of your keyboard? What are the things on your desk aside from your computer? Do you see a pen, notebooks, or paper? Then, as you start typing, pay attention to your fingers. What are the sensations that you feel each time you hit your fingers on the keyboard? Are your fingers stiff? Do you feel pain or discomfort? Then, notice the sound of the keyboard as you press each key. Then, look at the screen and watch carefully as each letter starts appearing on your screen.

Many people avoid this mindfulness technique because they think that this will interfere with their work and will negatively affect their productivity, but it is actually the opposite. This practice will help improve your productivity and it allows you to work a lot faster than usual.

3. Opening a door

Whenever you open the door, take the time to examine the color and the texture of the door. Then, notice the color and the texture of the doorknob. How does it feel? Does it feel warm or cold? Can you feel the sweat in your palm as you touch the doorknob? Then, pay attention to the sound it makes when you twist the knob and open the door. This activity may look silly, but this will allow you to pay attention to simple day-to-day tasks such as opening the door.

4. People watching.

One way to practice meditation in your daily life is people watching. You can sit on a park bench and observe the people passing in front of you (just glance at them; do not stare). What's the color of that person's shirt, hair, or skin? Is he tall or short? How does he walk? Does it seem like he's in a hurry?

This exercise allows you to practice mindfulness in your daily life. This exercise also enhances your cognitive functions and observation skills that can improve your decision-making skills and productivity.

You can practice mindfulness in every aspect of your life. You can be mindful while you're watching TV, talking to your friends, drinking beer, cooking, and even while you are cleaning. When you practice mindfulness in everything that you do, you'll feel more immersed into your every experience. You feel more vibrant and alive. You also become more aware of the things that are happening around you. So you won't feel that you're just someone who's drifting mindlessly through life.

Conclusion

Thank you again for downloading this book!

I hope this book was able to help you to jumpstart your meditation practice.

The next step is to keep doing the steps and techniques that are contained in this book. Remember that mindfulness is not something that you can master in just a couple of weeks. So, if you have to be patient with yourself. Do not give up and just keep on practicing. Soon enough, you'll reap the full benefits of your mindfulness practice. You'll have less stress and worries and the quality of your life will significantly improve. Once you have mastered your mindfulness practice, don't forget to share it with others.

Finally, if you enjoyed this book, then I'd like to ask you for a favor, would you be kind enough to leave a review for this book on Amazon? It'd be greatly appreciated!

Thank you and good luck!

Made in the USA
Middletown, DE
21 January 2019